His Green Eyes

Cheyenne Bluett

ISBN-13: 978-0-578-66775-1
Cover design by: 100 Covers
Printed in the United States of America

BOOKS BY THIS AUTHOR

Poetry

Bright Yellow Sunshine
Dark Blue Waves
The Moon Sends Her Love
Magic All Along
I Miss You Tonight

Paranormal Romance
(Pandora Bluett)

Wicked Transcendence

DEDICATION

This book is dedicated to my husband, Robert.

Thank you for being my muse and inspiration for this novel. I love you more than anything in this world, and I hope this shows you just how much you mean to me. Thank you for loving me unconditionally and giving me a love that is better than the movies.

I am yours forever.

TO THE READER

My hope for you
is that while you read
these poems and prose
of love and happiness,
you are filled with
a warm tingling in your soul
and a hug around your heart
that proves true love is real.

xoxo

There

is

nothing

more

beautiful

in

this

world

than

His

Green

Eyes.

HIS GREEN EYES

When I look at you
you make my heart sing.
I hope to never
lose this feeling.
I want to love you
forevermore.

DRUNK IN LOVE

Do you remember the night
when you had too much to drink
and you whispered secrets to me?
You had drunkenly breathed
"I love you."

I giggled
and reminded you that you were drunk.
You said that you knew that,
but it still was true,
so I whispered
"I love you, too."

HIS GREEN EYES

For so long
I wished
to find someone like you.
I wished on eyelashes
and ladybugs,
shooting stars
and dandelions
waiting for the day when
my wish would come true…
and it did when I met you.

HIS GREEN EYES

You turned my blue sky pink.

HIS GREEN EYES

You kissed me
and ever since then,
I believe in magic.

HIS GREEN EYES

Never stop
putting your hand
on the small of my back
and claiming me as yours:

                  Your Wife.

HIS GREEN EYES

810.6

I kissed you goodbye and you drove away.
Then I got on a plane
to go live my life
810.6 miles away.

Every time I did push ups
until my arms failed me
and questioned why I even left,
and wanted to quit,
I thought of you.

Even though you were 810.6 miles away.

Every time I cried myself to sleep
and felt the ache of loneliness
and wanted to quit,
I thought of you
and our future.

Wishing you weren't 810.6 miles away.

Every time I read your letters
and wanted to see you in person so badly
and wanted to quit,
I thought of you
and our future
and our future children.

And then that amazing day when
you came to see my graduate,
we hugged and kissed and

HIS GREEN EYES

I was so overjoyed.

I made it.
We made it.

The only thing left
was our future.

I did this for you,
for me,
for us—
and we made it
even though we were
810.6 miles apart.

HIS GREEN EYES

You are my rock.
I am your cloud.

> You hold me down
> and I make you float.

> > Without you, I'd be lost.
> > And without me, you'd be stuck.

HIS GREEN EYES

Your smile
shines brighter
than one hundred moons
gathered for a
wondrous awakening.

Your love
warms me
more one thousand suns
gathered for a
magnificent eclipse.

I love you
more than
all the infinite stars
shooting around the universe
in a skyrocketing frolic.

HIS GREEN EYES

I'll love you more
in a dirty yellow work shirt
than I'd ever love you
flawless in a tux.

HIS GREEN EYES

Kiss me every time
you leave the house
and kiss me every time
you want to leave.

Never leave me angry,
a kiss will make everything better.

HIS GREEN EYES

The way she laughs
makes my insides sparkle
more than a glass of champagne.

HIS GREEN EYES

I glance at the clock: 3:38am.
You yawn in the passenger seat.
We've been sitting in the car
for what seems like eons.
I ask if you are ready for me to leave.
You pull me close and whisper no.
I giggle as you nuzzle into my neck.
Is this love?

HIS GREEN EYES

The feeling of your hands
on my waist
and your soft kiss
on my forehead
make me feel so at ease, so loved.
How did I get so lucky?
Is this all a dream?
Will I wake up eventually?

Every kiss you planted on me

grew a daisy brighter than the last.

HIS GREEN EYES

Some days I wonder
how I got so lucky
to find someone like you.

> Other days I wonder
> how you got so lucky
> to find someone like me.

HIS GREEN EYES

Tell me you love me.
Tell me you love me so much.
Tell me you love me forever and ever.
Tell me you love me
and then tell me *again*.

HIS GREEN EYES

Lying in bed next to you
is my favorite place to be,
feeling your warm body
and your arms wrapped around me.
Snuggle me tight,
and let's fall asleep.

HIS GREEN EYES

Your skin is so soft
as I caress your face
with my fingers.
Your hair is draping
over your green eyes,
which are gleaming
in the moonlight.
I could gaze into
them all night.

HIS GREEN EYES

I didn't fall in love with you
because of your delicate heart
or your sweet words.

I fell in love with you
because of the way
you held me tight
and still loved me,

even after I told you about
the years of abuse
and the frightening fears
stuck inside my mind.

LOVING YOU IN EVERY COLOR

RED

Red is I love you's
and red roses on a Tuesday.
Red is kiss me softly.
Red is the heat pumping through our veins.
Red is the shirt you wear out to dinner.
Red is loving you.

LOVING YOU IN EVERY COLOR

ORANGE

Orange is I love you's
and kittens snuggling on the couch.
Orange is your favorite color.
Orange is eating fruit.
Orange is you holding my hand
as we watch the sunset.
Orange is loving you.

LOVING YOU IN EVERY COLOR

YELLOW

Yellow is I love you's
and bees buzzing through our flowers.
Yellow is our home.
Yellow is the sunshine.
Yellow is the happiness
I feel when we are together.
Yellow is loving you.

LOVING YOU IN EVERY COLOR

GREEN

Green is I love you's
and cuddling on a Saturday morning.
Green is hold me close.
Green is the color of your eyes.
Green is the grass on which
we picnic in the summer.
Green is loving you.

LOVING YOU IN EVERY COLOR

BLUE

Blue is I love you's
and tissues when you are feeling sick.
Blue is my favorite color.
Blue is our last name.
Blue is the ocean,
my favorite place to travel with you.
Blue is loving you.

LOVING YOU IN EVERY COLOR

VIOLET

Violet is I love you's
and eating dinner way too late at night.
Violet is giggling with you.
Violet is lavender-scented candles.
Violet is watching the stars with you
and pointing out constellations.
Violet is loving you.

HIS GREEN EYES

Radiantly handsome, my husband.
Oh my goodness. I love you so much!
Be mine forever?
Be mine for always?
I will be
Eternally yours.

Robbie

HIS GREEN EYES

I am addicted
to the way
you kiss me
good morning.

HIS GREEN EYES

Skip work today.
Lay in bed with me.
There will always be another workday
but there may never be
another day spent with me.
Let's cuddle and smooch
and giggle and sleep.
Who cares about work?
Just love me.

HIS GREEN EYES

I will
forever cherish
the day
you came
into my life
and stayed.

You made me
fall in love
just by
loving me
exactly
how I needed.

HIS GREEN EYES

You put the stars in the sky,
and love in my heart.
You may not realize this,
but you do-
and I will always be here,
waiting for you.

HIS GREEN EYES

LOVING YOU

Oh, how I never want to stop
dancing in this kitchen with you.
Twirl me around
until you can't spin me anymore.
Your smile brightens up the room
and I am dazzled.

HIS GREEN EYES

I couldn't tell
if I was drunk
on the wine
or your cologne.

HIS GREEN EYES

Honestly…
I don't know
how I ever lived
without you.

I don't know how I ever thought
my soulmate was ever someone
other than you.

The day we met,
the day you came into my life
was the day everything finally made sense.

You are more than I ever dreamed
and yet, you are just what I need.

Thank you for choosing me,
even though I am difficult most of the time
because I could never live this life
without you.

I love you so much.

HIS GREEN EYES

Your smile brightens up my days
as does your laugh, your eyes.
Your hugs leave me breathless
and your kisses give me butterflies.

HIS GREEN EYES

It's so unbelievable
and wonderful
that I was born
at the right time
and the right place
to end up meeting
and marrying you.

HIS GREEN EYES

Hold me close,
feel me breathe.
Don't let go
or ever leave.

HIS GREEN EYES

FRECKLES

I am so incredibly jealous
of all the angels that have kissed your face.

HIS GREEN EYES

My whole life
I've been told
that fairytales do not exist.
Well, my darling,
they must've never met you.

HIS GREEN EYES

Men are so tough
until they want to be the little spoon.
Yes, honey, I will hold you.

WHAT I WISH YOUNG ME WOULD'VE KNOWN.

Wait.
Please, just wait.
I know you think you can't find a man
who is perfect for you in every way,
but I am here to tell you,
wait.
You can AND you will.
He is out there.

Don't settle for the boys
who scream at you
and abuse you for sport.

Instead, wait for the man
who speaks softly and affectionately,
who builds you up and helps you grow.
He is out there, and he is waiting for you too.

I know it may take a while.
and things may get bumpy.
You may think he isn't coming
but he is.
I promise.

Wait for the right man.
And you will know when it is him.
And it will all be worth it.

HIS GREEN EYES

If there ever comes a time
when my eyesight fails me
and I become blind,
just know I could never
forget your sweet face,
for when I close my eyes
it is etched inside my mind.

HIS GREEN EYES

People always told me,
"You will know when you know",
and I always thought that was such a lie.
It used to keep me up at night,
anxious questions running through my mind.
How will I know when he is The One?
I've been wrong before.
How will I know that he loves me unconditionally
and won't stop after he finds another?
How will I know that he will want me forever?
That's such a long time…

I fear I'll pick the wrong man
and be forced to live a life
unhappy and unloved.
How will I know?
How will I know?

And then one day.

You showed up.

Arriving in my life.

And I knew instantly.

HIS GREEN EYES

If I could
kiss you
every moment,
every second,
every minute
of every day,
I would.

HIS GREEN EYES

Sparkly and radiant
is the diamond on my finger,
almost as beautiful
as the twinkling of the stars
on that night when you asked me
to be forever yours.

HIS GREEN EYES

You came into
my complicated life
and made everything seem so simple.

JAVA LOVA

Coffee.
Mmmm.
My favorite.
I cup the warm mug in my hands
and take a sip.
The only thing warmer
than this vanilla java
is the way you are smiling at me.

HIS GREEN EYES

The colors in her cheeks
make the sunrise look dull.

HIS GREEN EYES

I want to sleep
but I am afraid
that when I wake
you will dissipate
with my dreams.

HIS GREEN EYES

I am your wife.
You are my husband.
That sounds so sexy.

Say it again.

HIS GREEN EYES

Kiss me under
the moonlight
tonight
and kiss me under
the sunrise tomorrow.

You are unable
to say
goodbye
if your lips
are eternally
dancing with mine.

LETTERS

Letters are the only things
that are keeping me going.
I read your scrawl hungrily,
savoring each word.

You tell me
you love me,
about life back home,
and about how it's not the same
since I've been gone.

I miss home.
I miss you.
I'm counting down the days
until I see you again.

HIS GREEN EYES

I believe in soulmates.
And I know
without a doubt
you are mine.

HIS GREEN EYES

I was scared
when you asked
where that scar was from.

How do I tell you
about the endless nights,
the many cuts
I drew on myself
to feel something, anything.

I whispered the words,
told you what I had done,
and bowed my head in defeat.

To my surprise,
you kissed my wrist,
and promised me
from now on,
kisses would be
the only new marks
being planted on my wrists.

HIS GREEN EYES

Love isn't always
fireworks and rainbows.
Sometimes it is
monsoons and thunderstorms.
You just have to find
the person who will
choose you through
the fury
to get to paradise.

THE NIGHT WE MET

Sitting on your lap
and talking for hours
was definitely the highlight of my night.
If only we could
have stayed together
until the darkness turned to light.

You were but a stranger,
but I longed to know every part of you.
I had learned your name,
and you learned mine.

When we said goodbye,
my name sounded as if
it belonged on your lips.

HIS GREEN EYES

You take away my pain
and heal my wounds
with your everlasting love.

You were the prescription
I did not know
my soul needed.

HIS GREEN EYES

I could write
infinite poems
all about the way I feel
when he smiles at me.

HIS GREEN EYES

I wear your heart
every day
in the little red ring
that you gave me.

HIS GREEN EYES

When you press
your forehead
against mine,
it's as if a channel flows through us,
connecting our hearts.

I feel so loved and protected
and oh so close to you.

THE MISSED CALL

I have only ever hated you
once in my life.

As you are reading this,
I am sure you are laughing,
because you know *exactly*
what day I am talking about.

The day you missed
my phone call in basic training.

But I have loved you every day since then.

HIS GREEN EYES

I want to sit in trees
and paint the leaves
with you.

Be with me through all changing seasons.

HIS GREEN EYES

You are the reason
that I am
so fabulously
happy.

HIS GREEN EYES

Your love is more precious to me
than diamonds or rubies.
Even when
you're being annoying
and all you want to do
is touch my boobies.

HIS GREEN EYES

I love you all the time.
Every single day.
Even when I don't like you,
I still love you.
Does that make sense?
Or am I crazy?

OUR WEDDING DAY

The best day of my life
was when I wore
that long blush dress
with ivory lace
adorning my bodice and train
that made me look like a princess.
No, wait, even better:
I looked like a bride.
I was a bride.
I was *your* bride.

In that beautiful church
with intricate stained-glass windows
you stood at the altar
wearing a tux-
the most handsome
I had ever seen you thus far.
The way you were beaming
at me walking down the aisle
was the best sight I had ever seen.

Whenever you vowed
in sickness and health,
for richer or poorer,
and pledged your faithfulness
to me,
my infinite adoration for you grew.

You chose me to be:
your fun side,
your best friend,

HIS GREEN EYES

your sweetheart,
your partner-in-crime,
and *your wife.*

I chose you to be:
my everything,
my best friend,
my rock,
my on-and-only,
and *my husband.*

And I cannot wait
to love you
and live this life
with you as one,
and Mr. & Mrs.
now,
forever,
and thereafter.

LOVING YOU IN MY FAVORITE PLACES

KINCAID

Kincaid is mudfest
and meeting you,
drunk on fruity drinks
and the smell of your cologne.
Smiling at each other
for the very first time.
I love you in Kincaid.

LOVING YOU IN MY FAVORITE PLACES

FT. JACKSON

Ft. Jackson is graduation
and a bright sunny day
and you driving states away
just to see me again.
Smiling at each other
for the first time in months.
I love you in Ft. Jackson.

LOVING YOU IN MY FAVORITE PLACES

ST. THOMAS

St. Thomas is tropical
and a warm summer breeze,
sipping on a banana daiquiri
and kissing on the beach.
Smiling at each other
after you proposed to me.
I love you in St. Thomas.

LOVING YOU IN MY FAVORITE PLACES

LURAY

Luray is honeymooning
with magnificent mountains in the sky
and captivating caverns
under our feet.
Smiling at each other
since we said I do last week.
I love you in Luray.

LOVING YOU IN MY FAVORITE PLACES

CHICAGO

Chicago is traffic
and walking hand in hand
down Michigan Avenue,
cheeks pink from the cold.
Smiling at each other,
even though our hands are frozen.
I love you in Chicago.

LOVING YOU IN MY FAVORITE PLACES

ATHENS

Athens is home
and cuddling on the couch
with our kitties and puppy
snoozing away.
Smiling at each other
in our home with our family.
I love you in Athens.

HIS GREEN EYES

Coffee mugs
& warm hugs.

        Singing birds
        & lovely words.

                The color blue
                & me & you.

       My favorite things.

HIS GREEN EYES

I get drunk
every time we kiss.
Your lips taste
like a wine
fermented just for me.

HIS GREEN EYES

I am so
thankful and grateful
that you chose me, too.

MY GARDENER

I never knew I needed a gardener
until you came into my life.
I didn't pay enough attention
to the flowers in my soul
to notice they were withering and unkempt.

Then you came along
and started watering my spirit daily
with kisses and love
and encouragement and cuddles,
and my flowers started blooming.

You gave me the courage
to slash out the weeds
and let myself blossom like never before.

Now I never fear of the petals falling off,
for they are flourishing more than they ever have...

and I owe it all to you.

HIS GREEN EYES

The way you smile
makes me believe
there is a God.

HIS GREEN EYES

My heart
longing for your presence
is beating intently because
I am thinking of you.
Oh, how I wish
I could see you,
touch you,
kiss you.

HIS GREEN EYES

When we are old and gray
and our children are grown
and our lives are almost done,
I hope you turn to me
and grin and say
"That was so much f*cking fun."

HIS GREEN EYES

Together we make
a color
no one else
could understand.

HIS GREEN EYES

Every time you compliment me
or tell me something sweet
I tattoo it in my memory.

some of my favorites –

You are perfectly imperfect.
The way you look,
the way you love,
the way you act & feel.
You're not perfect, but you're pretty close!

I would never leave you.
I will stay with you and do my best to make you happy.
I need you.
I am here forever.

I know I say it a lot,
but I love you so much!
I just want you to know without a doubt
that I love you with my whole heart!

HIS GREEN EYES

Send me a text.
Write me a letter.
Anything to know
that you're thinking of me.

HIS GREEN EYES

My only hope
is that my brain
never forgets
the way you sweet face
smiles when you dream.

HIS GREEN EYES

I would serenade you
with aged love songs
until my lungs gave out
if you'd let me…

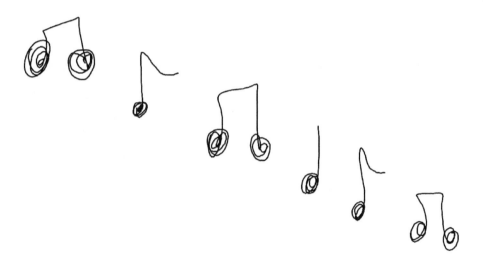

HIS GREEN EYES

With you I am happier
than a squirrel
who found a whole cob of corn!

HIS GREEN EYES

Dance with me.
Please dance with me.

Do you hear the jazz
coming from the bar?
Don't you see
I've worn my best dress?

Just grab my hand
and I will lead.

Kiss me under the moonlight tonight,
and dance with me.

HIS GREEN EYES

The angels definitely
created us for each other.
How else
could you explain
how perfectly my head fits
cradled in your neck?

HIS GREEN EYES

I remember telling you
on our second date
that I was going to
marry you someday…
and look at us now.

HIS GREEN EYES

On the days where I
am anxious beyond belief
or so depressed I
can't bear to face the day,
you are there to calm my worries
and make me feel better.
You get me out of bed,
cook me breakfast,
rub my feet,
and remind me how much you love me.
You take my Armageddon
and turn it into Heaven.

HIS GREEN EYES

As I lay here
with your chest
under my ear,
I am soothed
by the sound
of your heartbeat.

This reassuring sound
proves to me
that this love,
this perfect life with you,
is really true.

HIS GREEN EYES

You sleep on the couch
all alone
while you wait for me
to come home
because you cannot imagine
going to bed without me.

HIS GREEN EYES

I know I always write
about the way he kisses me
and about his beautiful green eyes,
but if you only knew
the feeling of his soft lips
caressing mine, embracing me
or
the way his eyes light up
when he sees me from across the room,
then that would be all
you thought of too.

HIS GREEN EYES

ACKNOWLEDGEMENTS

I have so many people I want to thank!
In no particular order:

Thank you to my wonderful parents. You have encouraged my writing ever since I was a little kid & I am so incredibly grateful for you!

My amazing, every-good-word-in-the-dictionary, handsome-as-hell husband, Robbie. Thank you for supporting me in following my dreams and pushing me to publish my work!

Thank you to Tara, who has shown me the importance of being vulnerable. I did it!

Thank you to my amazing friends & family who have supported me every step of the way. You know who you are! I could not have done any of this without you!

Thank you to my launch team! Your support means so much to me and I thank you for helping me get my book off to a great start!

And last, but not least, YOU! Thank you to you for taking the time to read this book & support my words.

HIS GREEN EYES

ABOUT THE AUTHOR:

Cheyenne Bluett is the author of the many Amazon bestselling poetry books. She was born and raised in Illinois, where she still currently resides with her husband, daughter, and fur-children. When she is not writing or working on one of her ten thousand projects, you can find her teaching preschool, reading a good book with a hot chocolate, or rewatching Twilight for the thousandth time.

HIS GREEN EYES

CAN YOU HELP?

Thank You For Reading My Book!

I really appreciate all of your feedback, and I love hearing what you have to say.

Please leave me a review on Amazon letting me know what you thought of the book.

Thank you so much!

Xoxo,

Cheyenne

Printed in Great Britain
by Amazon

23121733R00067